Studying Dolphins

By Eliza Webb

This beautiful place is called Alphabet Cove.

Alphabet Cove is home to lots of marine animals, like whales, dolphins, sharks and elephant seals.

Steph's job is to study the animal life in the cove.
She tracks the animals and makes notes about them.

Today, Steph takes her boat out to check on some dolphins.

Steph

A few dolphin groups swim around Alphabet Cove.

A group of dolphins is called a pod.

The waves are not big so Steph can see well enough to spot a pod!

Steph drives her boat closer to the dolphin pod.

The dolphins know Steph, so they swim close to the boat.

She makes notes about the dolphin fins she can see.

Each dolphin fin is different.

The fins tell Steph which dolphin is which.
She knows all the dolphins in this pod!

One of the young dolphins in this pod is an orphan.
Steph calls him Baby Phil.
His smiling face always makes Steph laugh.

Steph thought that Baby Phil might have a tough life without his mum, but he is doing well.

Next, Steph listens to the dolphins with this device.

She puts it into the sea and listens for dolphin noises.

The noises are the sound of dolphins talking to each other!

The dolphins talk with buzzes and clicks.

Sometimes, old fishing nets can trap dolphins, so Steph scans the cove for rubbish.

Then she takes some photos of all the dolphins in the pod.

The dolphins jump and dive and show off for Steph!

The sea is getting a bit rough now, so the boat rocks.

When she has enough photos, Steph heads back to land.

Back on land, Steph uses a phone app to post the photos online.

Then she makes a graph about the dolphins' health.

Steph helps us find out lots of things about dolphins.

The pod in Alphabet Cove is doing well!

CHECKING FOR MEANING

1. How does Steph know which dolphin is which? *(Literal)*
2. What two things does Steph do after she heads back to land? *(Literal)*
3. Why might it be helpful for Steph to make a graph about the dolphins' health? *(Inferential)*
4. Is Steph's job important? Why? *(Evaluative)*

EXTENDING VOCABULARY

orphan	Which letters in the word *orphan* make the /f/ sound? What is an orphan?
device	What is a device? What is another word the author could have used instead of *device*?
rough	What sound do the letters *gh* make together? What is the opposite of the word *rough*?

MOVING BEYOND THE TEXT

1. Would you like to do Steph's job? Why?
2. Dolphins can swim with their top fin sticking out of the water. What other animal might a dolphin be mistaken for in the water?
3. Steph works in the dolphins' natural habitat. Why is it important to study animals in their natural habitats?
4. What do people who work near water need to do to stay safe?

TIME TO WRITE

Write a short diary entry from Steph's point of view about your day as you check on the dolphins.